# My Counting Book

by Don L. Curry

**Consultant:**
Johanna Kaufman,
Math Learning/
Resource Coordinator
of the Dalton School

PEACH PLAINS SCHOO
Library Media Center
Grand Haven, MI 49417

Capstone Curriculum Publishing
Mankato, Minnesota

# 1

I see one polar bear sleeping in the snow.

1 polar bear

**1** 2 3 4 5 6 7 8 9 10

I see two hippopotamuses
swimming in the river.

2 hippopotamuses

# 3

I see three
kangaroos
standing in
the outback.

4

# 4

## 4 dolphins

I see four dolphins leaping through the waves.

# 5

I see five cheetahs resting on a hilltop.

1 2 3 4 **5** 6 7 8 9 10

I see six puppies sitting on a log.

**6**

**6 puppies**

1 2 3 4 5 **6** 7 8 9 10

# 7

I see seven zebras drinking with the herd.

I see eight horses galloping across the field.

8 horses

# 9

I see nine bison grazing on the plains.

**9 bison**

1 2 3 4 5 6 7 8 **9** 10

# 10

I see ten turtles lying in the sunlight.

**10 turtles**

# 1

How many do
you see?

Count the pandas
eating bamboo
leaves.

**1** 2 3 4 5 6 7 8 9 10

Count the piglets sleeping in the bucket.

2

2 piglets

# 3

Count the bunnies hiding under the flowers.

3 bunnies

# 4

## 4 chimpanzees

Count the chimpanzees eating fruit on the savannah.

# 5

## 5 prairie dogs

Count the prairie dogs sitting in the sun.

1 2 3 4 **5** 6 7 8 9 10

Count the giraffes walking with the herd.

6 giraffes

1   2   3   4   5   **6**   7   8   9   10

# 7

Count the elephants crossing the stream.

Count the sea lions barking on the rocky shore.

8 sea lions

# 9

Count the gazelles grazing in the valley.

**9 gazelles**

1 2 3 4 5 6 7 8 **9** 10

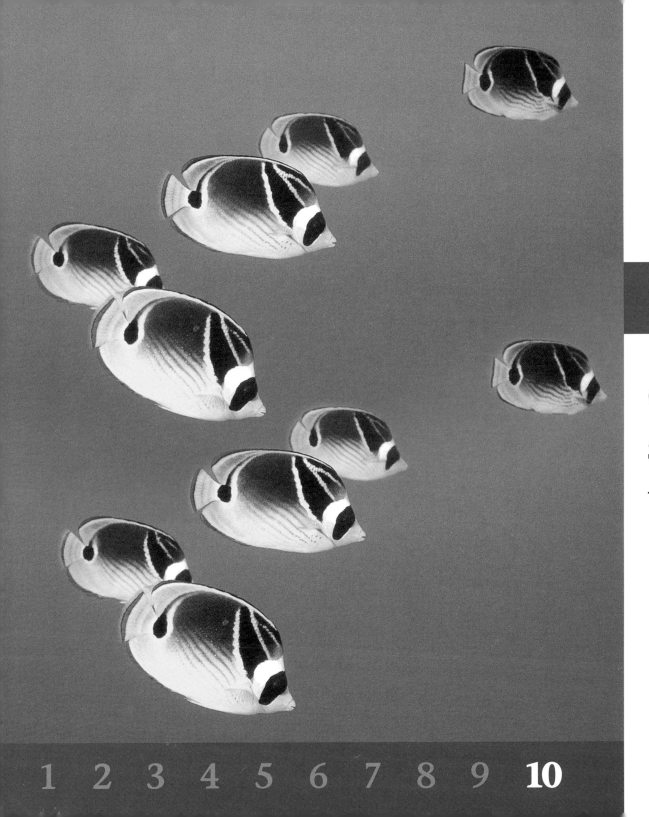

# 10

Count the fish
swimming in
the ocean.

1 2 3 4 5 6 7 8 9 **10**

# How many animals do you see?

One panda

Two piglets

Three bunnies

Four chimpanzees

Five prairie dogs

1 2 3 4 5 6 7 8 9 10

Six giraffes

Seven elephants

Eight sea lions

Nine gazelles

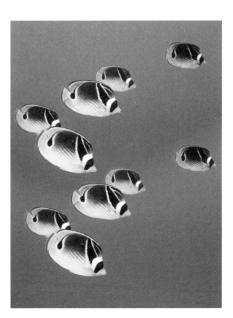

Ten fish

1 2 3 4 5 6 7 8 9 10

# How many animals do you see?

One polar bear

Two hippopotamuses

Three kangaroos

Four dolphins

Five cheetahs

1 2 3 4 5 6 7 8 9 10

Six puppies

Seven zebras

Eight horses

Nine bison

Ten turtles

**1 2 3 4 5 6 7 8 9 10**

# Note To Teachers and Parents

*My Counting Book* walks children through the world of animals while building mastery of basic counting skills. The combination of full-color photographs and numeric facts, as well as locational and animal-specific vocabulary, and a glossary filled with animal facts makes this book an excellent cross-curricular learning/teaching tool.

The real-life photographs, new vocabulary, and animal facts encourage lively discussions that develop oral language skills and extend science concepts, while developing counting skills. In addition, the list of web sites, the bibliography, and a hands-on project bring this book's information to learners of all styles.

# Hands-On Projects

## *My Animal Counting Book*

Invite children to create their own counting books. Set up a 14-page booklet by folding a stack of 11" x 14" sheets of paper in half and stapling them together at the fold. Invite children to write the numbers 0 through 10 on the outside upper corner of each page. Remind them that a book has a cover where they write the name of the book and the name of the author. Once their books have a cover and numbered pages, invite children to use their drawings or photographs from magazines and web sites to illustrate the number on each page. Have **My Counting Book** on display for children to refer to as they work.

## *Counting Animals*

**Materials:** plastic animals in sets of 10
index cards with numbers and symbols 0 through 10

Invite partners to play a counting game. Give one child 10 plastic animals. Give the other child in the pair a set of index cards with the numbers 0 through 10 printed on one side and a matching number of circles on the back.

The child with the flash cards randomly holds up an index card showing his or her partner the numeral. The second child in the pair then lays out that number of plastic animals. The child with the flash cards makes sure the number of circles matches the number of plastic animals the partner has placed on the table. If the amounts are equal, they trade roles.

# Internet Sites

## Animal Information Database
http://www.seaworld.org/infobook.html

## Homework Central
http://www.homeworkcentral.com

## The National Zoo's Photo Gallery
http://www.si.edu/natzoo/photos/phoset.htm

## Quillio the Hedgehog's Online Zoo
http://members.tripod.com/~Quillio/

## Really Wild Animals
http://www.nationalgeographic.com/features/97/rwa/

# Books About Animals

Donnelly, Jane. *Mighty Giants of the Wild.* New York: Simon & Schuster, 1996.

Jeunesse, Gallimard and Pascale de Bourgoing. *Dogs.* New York: Scholastic, 1999.

Lambert, David. *The Children's Animal Atlas.* Millbrook, CT: The Millbrook Press, 1991.

Ling, Mary. *See How They Grow: Pigs.* New York: DK Publishing, 1993.

Marzollo, Jean. *Ten Cats Have Hats.* New York: Scholastic, 1994.

Pfeffer, Wendy. *What's It Like to Be a Fish?* New York: HarperCollins, 1996.

Schlein, Miriam. *More Than One.* New York: Greenwillow Books, 1996.

Walker, Sally. *Rhinos.* New York: Carolrhoda, 1996.

# Glossary

## Koala

- Koalas belong to the *Phascolarctidae* family

- Koalas may grow to 2.6 ft. (780 mm) tall and weigh as much as 26.7 lbs. (12 kg)

- Koalas are found in the eucalyptus forests of the East Coast of Australia

## Polar Bear

- Polar bears belong to the *Ursidae* (bear) family; there are nine types of bears

- Polar bears can grow to 9 ft. (2.7 m) tall; have wide heads, large bodies, heavy paws, and are covered with long, thick white fur, even on the bottoms of their paws

- Polar bears live primarily on sheets of floating ice along the coast of the Arctic Ocean

## Hippopotamus

- Hippopotamuses belong to the *Hippopotamidae* family.

- Hippopotamuses may grow to weigh 4 tons (3,628.8 kgs), grow to a length of 14 ft. (4.2 m), and stand 5 ft. (1.5 m) tall

- The hippopotamus is found in and around the rivers of Eastern and Central Africa

## Kangaroo *(Eastern Gray)*

- Eastern gray kangaroos belong to the *Macropodidae* family

- Eastern gray kangaroos can grow to heights over 6 ft. (2 m), weigh more than 200 lbs. (444.4 kgs), and can jump 26 ft. (8 m) in a single bound at high speed

- Eastern gray kangaroos are found in Australia

## Dolphin *(Spotted)*

- Spotted dolphins belong to the *Delphinidae* (small-toothed whales) family

- Spotted dolphins are mammals that can grow up to 13 ft. (3.7 m) long, weigh up to 450 lbs. (204.5 kgs), and can swim as fast as 25 mph (990 kph)

- Spotted dolphins inhabit the temperate and subtropical waters of the Atlantic ocean

## Cheetah

- Cheetahs are members of the *Felidae* (cat) family

- Cheetahs can grow to 7 ft. (2.1 m) long, 30 in. (75 cm) tall, weigh as much as 140 lbs. (63.6 kg), and can run as fast as 70 mph (112 kph)

- Cheetahs are found on the open savannahs of the African continent, south of the Sahara Desert

## Puppy *(Irish Setter)*

- Irish setters are members of the *Canidae* family

- Irish setters have an orange-red coat, can grow to 27 in. (69 cm) tall and weigh as much as 70 lbs. (32 kg)

- Irish setters are domesticated dogs and are found in most places around the world

## Zebra

- Zebras are members of the *Equidae* (horse) family

- Zebras have varying arrangements of dark stripes on their heads, bodies, legs, and tails and may grow to 55 in. (140 cm) tall

- Zebras are found on the grassy African flatlands, from Southern Ethiopia to the Cape of Good Hope

## Horse *(Arabian)*

- Arabian horses are members of the *Equidae* (horse) family

- Arabian horses may grow to 15.2 hands in height and weigh as much as 1,000 lbs. (454.5 kg)

- Arabian horses are found throughout the world

## Bison *(American)*

- American bison are members of the *Bovidae* family

- American bison can grow to 6 ft. (1.8 m) tall, 11 ft. (3.3 m) in length, and weigh as much as 2200 lbs. (990 kg)

- American bison are found in National parks and reserves throughout North America

## Turtle *(Painted)*

- Painted turtles are members of the *Emydidae* family

- Painted turtles are brightly marked, have a relatively flat shell that can grow to 7.2 in. (18 cm) long with red and yellow markings on a black or brown background

- Painted turtles are found in North America, from southern Canada to northern Mexico

## Panda *(Giant)*

- Giant pandas belong to the *Ursidae* (bear) family

- Giant pandas may grow to 5 ft. (1.5 m) and weigh up to 350 lbs. (160 kgs)

- Giant pandas are found in bamboo forests in the mountains of central China and eastern Tibet

## Piglet *(pig)*

- Pigs or hogs are part of the *Suida* family (even-toed, hoofed animals)

- Pigs vary in size from the pygmy hog at 1 ft. (30 cm) tall and 13 lbs. (5.85 kg) to the domestic hog at 2 ft. (60 cm) tall and weighing as much as 2500 lbs. (1125 kg)

- Pigs are found throughout the world

## Rabbit *(Cottontail)*

- Cottontail rabbits are members of the *Leporidae* family

- Cottontail rabbits have long ears, long hind legs, a short white tail, and can grow to 18 in. (45 cm) long and weigh up to 3 lbs. (13.5 kg)

- Cottontail rabbits are found throughout North America

## Chimpanzee

- Chimpanzees are members of the *Pongidae* family

- Chimpanzees may grow to 4.5 ft. (1.35 m) tall and weigh up to 110 lbs. (49.5 kgs)

- Chimpanzees are found in the rain forests and wet savannahs of Africa

## Prairie Dog *(Black-tailed)*

- Black-tailed prairie dogs are members of the *Scuridae* family

- Black-tailed prairie dogs can grow to 1 ft. (30 cm) long with a 4 in. (10 cm) tail and can weigh up to 5 lbs. (2.25 kg)

- Black-tailed prairie dogs are found on the prairies and semi-deserts of the northwestern United States

## Giraffe

- The giraffe is a member of the *Giraffidae* family

- The giraffe is the tallest living animal at 20 ft. (5.9 m). The front legs may grow to 10 ft. (2.9 m) in length, the neck to 7 ft. (2.1 m), and the tongue to 1.5 ft. (.45 m)

- Giraffes live in small herds and are found only on the plains of eastern Africa

## Elephant *(African)*

- African elephants are members of the *Elephantidae* family

- African elephants are the largest living land mammals growing as big as 24 ft. (7.2 m) long, 12 ft. (3.6 m) tall and weighing up to 17,000 lbs. (7650 kg)

- African elephants are found on the savannah grassland and forests of the African continent south of the Sahara

## Sea Lion *(California)*

• California sea lions are members of the *Otariidae* family

• California sea lions have streamlined bodies with thick layers of fat, flippers, and thick, hairy coats

• California sea lions are found in and out of the water along the coasts of Australia and the west coast of the United States

## Gazzelle *(Grant's)*

• Grant's gazzelles are members of the *Bovidae* family

• Grant's gazzelles can grow to 6 ft. (1.8 m) long and weigh up to 100 lbs. (45 kg)

• Grant's gazzelles are found in the semi-desert to open savannahs of Tanzania, Kenya, Ethiopia, Somalia, and Sudan

## Fish *(Raccoon Butterflyfish)*

• Raccoon butterflyfish are members of the *Chaetodontidae* (Butterflyfish) family

• Raccoon butterflyfish are nocturnal (active at night), ray-finned fish that can grow to 8 in. (20 cm) long

• Raccoon butterflyfish are found in the Indian, Pacific, and Southeast Atlantic Oceans

# Index

A+ Books are published by Capstone Press
P.O. Box 669, Mankato, Minnesota 56002
http://www.capstone-press.com

EDITORIAL CREDITS:
Susan Evento, Managing Editor/Product Development; Don L. Curry, Senior Editor; Jannike Hess, Designer; Kimberly Danger and Heidi Schoof, Photo Researchers; Content Consultant: Johanna Kaufman

LIBRARY OF CONGRESS CATALOGING-IN-PUBLICATION DATA:
Curry, Don L.
    My Counting Book by Don L. Curry; consultant, Johanna Kaufman
        p. cm.
    Includes bibliographical references and index.
    Summary: Invites the reader to count a variety of animals engaged
    in different activities.
    ISBN 0-7368-7041-5 (hard)     ISBN 0-7368-7051-2 (paper)
    1. Counting–Juvenile literature. [1. Counting. 2. Animals.] I. Title

QA133.C87 1999
513.211–dc21
[E]                                                                99-049696

PHOTO CREDITS:
Cover: Tom Brakefield/Bruce Coleman Inc.; Title Page: Doug Perrine/Innerspace Visions; Page 2: Photri Inc.; Page 3: Tom Brakefield/Bruce Coleman Inc.; Page 4: Inga Spence/Tom Stack and Assoc.; Page 5: Robert L. Pitman/Innerspace Visions; Page 6: F. Polking/Bruce Coleman, Inc.; Page 7: Photri Inc.; Page 8: Clem Haagner/Bruce Coleman, Inc.; Page 9: Kathy Hamer/Unicorn Stock Photos; Page 10: David Young/Tom Stack & Assoc.; Page 11: Cheryl A. Ertelt; Page 12: Robert C. Simpson/Uniphoto; Page 13: Ernest James/Index Stock; Page 14: Gay Bumgarner/Photo Network; Page 15: K & K Ammann/Bruce Coleman Inc.; Page 16: Scott Nielsen/Bruce Coleman Inc.; Page 17: Bob & Ann Simpson/Visuals Unlimited; Page 18: Bob & Ann Simpson/Visuals Unlimited; Page 19: Dave B. Fleetham/Visuals Unlimited; Page 20: Rowan Edmanson/International Stock; Page 21: Doug Perrine/Innerspace Visions; Page 22: (left to right top) Robert C. Simpson/Uniphoto, Ernest James/Index Stock; Gay Bumgarner/Photo Network (bottom left to right) K & K Ammann/Bruce Coleman Inc., Scott Nielsen/Bruce Coleman Inc.; Page 23: (top left to right) Bob & Ann Simpson/Visuals Unlimited; David Young/Tom Stack & Assoc., Doug Perrine/Innerspace Visions.